DAMN

Z.C. Angel

Second Edition

ISBN 978-1-105-68288-9

For Wela and Welo.

Acknowledgements

Thanks all of you out there that love me unconditionally.

Jorge you will always be my happiness. (bitch-slap)

I want to also thank bingo players and scratch-off players. I too want to thank Welo: my idol. Wela: my friend, mother, grandmother, and most importantly, my savior. Anthony: my only brother. Remember it's you and me, no matter what. Thanks to my Oviedo family. (You know who you are.) Thanks to Roy, Zacsi, Sam, and Chewie for giving me a new family. Papi, for loving me for being me, in the end.

Madison, the DIVA!

Wall-e, my laptop, for being there with me on endless nights. Last but not least: G and R, my deviant helpers.

fluffy not fat

I always knew I was different.

Not like alien different; or curly hair
different.

Just different.

My hazel eyes wandered a lot,
especially in gym class towards Jacob's
muscles, Ryan's ass, Kyle's wet body,
and Pablo's abs. I thought it was
because of the shape of my body, but it
wasn't until later on that I truly found
out why.

Gay?

Me?

Why?

Not only was I being called donut, because I volunteered at Dunkin Donuts.

Now this. I was scared.

Damn!

sweet pea and hello kitty

At the age of fifteen, I thought I found love.

"Phil said he liked you?" Sherelle whispered as she checked under the stalls to see if anyone was in there.

"Yes! Can you fucking believe it?"

"No." Sherelle said as she entered a stall.

"I know you hate him, girl, but it's not like he plays on your side." I said as I applied lip gloss while I stared at the cracked bathroom mirror.

"Caleb, you know I like you, right?"

"Duh! Yeah and this lip gloss by the way is the bomb!"

I took out my Sweet Pea body splash and sprayed the bathroom. Not only was the mix of menstrual blood, shit and cigarette smoke overpowering, Sherelle had to light up a joint while she was taking a shit and I sure as hell was not going to smell like slut. After thirty squirts of Sweet Pea I put the bottle in my Hello Kitty book bag.

"Not the problem. And yes the lip gloss is all that and a bag of tricks, but Phil isn't the one for you."

"Sherelle, can't you just be happy for me?"

"I can't!"

"What the fuck? I thought you were my b.f.f.u.d."

"Yeah until one of us dies but I'm going out with him. Sorry, Caleb."

"I'm sorry, too! You're a fucking

slut and your lip gloss is in the trash on top of a pad!"

"Oh if I wasn't taking a shit, I would kick your ass!"

"You're full of it! Wipe thoroughly!" I stormed out of the bathroom and ran into Phil in the hallway.

"Hey Caleb."

"Fuck you Phil!" I yelled to him on my way to 3rd period.

The funny thing is that Sherelle did wipe thoroughly and later on that day at our school swim meet she lost her

virginity with Phil. That bitch.

good versus god

Things got a little worse that night. My father decided to show us films from his church retreat in Brazil. While the film was rolling, I remember watching the sunset out the window. A moment I'll never forget. Off in the distance a cactus stood alone in the vast desert area. The silhouette of the cactus against the sun rising looked like the devil's horns. My father also rose with the sun and stood in front of the cactus.

The devil.

Lucifer himself.

I hated the butterflies this demonic excuse for a father left in my stomach after every confrontation. Not sexual, just emotional and physical. A father never should lay a hand on his child. I guess no one told this to "Lucifather" that son of a bitch. Wait, I take that back, Wela's not a bitch.

I was neglected because of my uniqueness. My name is Caleb, but in my home, a safe haven, "Sissy" became my name. Little girl this, sissy that. The walls embraced me more than his hellish arms ever could.

He had no heart, loved to taunt, thought the world revolved around him and always had the house at 96 degrees in the summer because if the house got real cold the devil would enter. News Flash: he already lived there.

Casa Rivera.

Owner: Ricardo a.k.a "Lucif-ather".

Welcome to hell. Albuquerque, New Mexico.

make a wish foundation

kids have it better

I celebrate everyone's birthday the way I'd like to celebrate mine, but when it's my b-day, no one's home. Especially on my sixteenth. There I was in my "sanctuary" one day before Halloween in 1999, hoping for a surprise birthday party.

I'm all alone.

Every year, I kept on wishing that it'd be different.

My idea of a beautiful birthday back then would be exactly like this.

On my special day people would come together, I'd receive joyous calls, and knocks on the door from lost friends.

A big banquet hall with tables full of champagne, I mean apple cider glasses.

Streamers. A banner with 'Happy 16th Birthday Beautiful!'.

A buffet table full of my favorite treats. Lemonhead Cupcakes, white-chocolate covered bananas, Swedish fish, caramel apples, rock candy, and a bowl of raspberry Kool-Aid. At the center of the buffet table would be my huge yellow cupcake-cake with butterflies for candles.

The guest all spruced up, while they wait anxiously for the guest of honor.

MOI!

If only it were true.

Instead, I'd be in my room in a house of strangers who were always out on my special day.

In front of me in a plastic

container is a slice of 'Death by

Chocolate' cake.

Gods damn it!

plastic fantastic

The only one who would really show up to my b-days then and because she had no other choice was Madison. She's been with me since the age of 12. I stole her from my cousin Taylor-Anne, who was five at the time and to this day she's still looking for her.

No one ever came up to my room so Madison hid on my bookshelf every day.

A Barbie doll. I like her so much; yes she still is with me years later. She listened to me, she'd let me comb her hair every day. I wished I had long curls like her back then and my wish came true a year later. My dark brown curls fashioned my head. Madison is the first girl I ever saw naked and didn't throw up on her caramel colored feet. That meant something right?

"Caleb don't worry, I got you a present."

"Oh you did and what's that?"

Madison had a pink box with a blue note card on it. The card read "Happy B-Day! Love M."

I hugged her, not too tight; I didn't want to wrinkle her new gold party dress.

"Thanks, Madison."

I opened the box and inside was another outfit for Madison; A yellow polka-dotted tank with jean daisy dukes and clear sandals.

"You shouldn't have."

The door downstairs opened and

in walked Lucif-ather and his followers, step-bitch and Nathan, my brother. No one came upstairs to check on me. Remember, it was my birthday.

Two hours went by and Madison was enjoying her new outfit.

All of a sudden there was a knock on my door.

"Madison, hide!"

"Hello!" Madison screamed back.

"Oh."

I put her on the shelf and

answered my door.

Nathan handed me a wrapped silver box.

"What's this?" I asked him as he walked towards his room down the hall.

"A gift Wela sent you." He turned around and faced me. "By the way Happy Birthday, faggot."

He smirked and headed into his room, slammed the door and blasted Josh Groban.

I closed my bedroom door and brushed off his comment.

A gift from Wela.

"What's that?" Madison asks me as she jumped down from the shelf, landing softly on my Felix the cat cover.

"Wela sent me a gift." I looked at her in shock.

"I'm glad it's from her and not your brother." Madison said as she applied apple flavored lip-gloss on her perfect lips. "Want some?"

"No thanks but do you want to help me open my grandmother's gift?"

"Can't, that's your moment."

Madison looked at herself in the mirror.

I opened the gift and to my surprise it was Madison in the box. New hairstyle, new clothes, shoes, accessories and bathing suit.

"Madison, it's you!"

"What?" Madison turned around and was in shock.

I tuned out Madison and just stared at the new doll. A new friend. Barbie. Not just a girl's best friend. The new doll's name ended up being Leila. "Don't you like that name?"

"Yep," answers Leila.

another minute (a.m.)

Two weeks later. I joined the high school's Gay-Straight Alliance, and met Billy Peterson. Billy's first words to me were, "You want my banana pudding?"

I was like, "Rude."

His laugh won me over. He seriously had banana pudding. I don't remember laughing so hard in my "so called" life. I love that show. I took the banana pudding from him and from that day on I never took my hazel eyes off of

his blue ones. He was my Jared Leto.

We formed a bond and decided

to become more than friends. Puerto-

Irish flavor we called ourselves.

My first relationship. Yeah!

Hold that thought.

Billy and Caleb equal an item.

My parents equal devoted

Baptists.

Junior Prom.

See my problem?

I lied and told my parents I had a

date, a girl date. Sherelle and I decided to rent a limo for the junior prom. My Lucifer, I mean father opposed at first, but decided later it was okay.

The limo picked up Billy first, and then me, Sherelle and Phil last.

Billy rang the doorbell at 8 p.m.

Waited for me until 8:15 p.m.

Kissed me at 8:17 p.m.

I was drop dead fuckable. See page 476 in the Spring J.C. Penny Catalogue.

Luckily my parents were asleep

at six, due to mass at 8 a.m. the next day.

That night Sherelle lost her virginity again and while I tried to lose mine, back at home of all places, I lost everything, unfortunately not my virginity.

3:08 a.m. Lucif-ather checked in on me.

We were caught kissing. Thank "whoever the fuck made humans", that my "dad" didn't walk in on us, how should I put this without grossing you out, doing the Cancer Horoscope sign.

Billy was thrown out.

"What in the Lord's name were you doing with him?" Lucif-ather said after he punched me in my face.

3:09 a.m.

"Nothing," I managed to get out.

"Don't lie to me!" He punched me in my chest.

I flew towards my lavender wall from the force of his punch and gasped for air. I looked over down the hallway and saw my brother. I mouthed 'help me'. He smirked and went into his room.

"Why do this to me? I'm your son?"

"Because in the eyes of the Lord you need to be punished!" Lucif-ather charged at me, kicked me, then the bee sting punches followed. I was told to repent or follow my demons to the street because no son of his was a sinner. I sat up against the wall with my busted lip and bruised body hoping that my step "mom" would walk in and hug me for once.

3:11 a.m.

3:13 a.m.

3:22 a.m.

She didn't.

I fake repented.

wela and me

On Sundays at church, I wished for death. The only problem about wishing for death was that I couldn't spend any more time with the coolest person ever.

Carmen Rivera, a.k.a. Wela.

Bingo nights were our thing. We

would leave the house two hours early just to get the best seats. Even if people were there before us, we would move their stuff and sit down.

An hour later, the regulars flooded the place.

Seven on the dot!, yelled the announcer.

"Apurate Puchito," said Wela. Puchito is my nickname.

There were 35 games in total including two jackpots. We looked forward to the intermissions. We would stuff our faces with random homemade items they offered. Rellenos de papa, pasteles, dulce de leche, hot dogs, flan, Cuban sandwiches, pernil, arroz con gandules, hush puppies and pickles. The nachos were our favorite.

Eight hours later, win or lose, we always left happy.

Wednesday and Friday nights were special.

Just her and me.

"O"

Other nights, I would "not lie" and tell my parents that I had study groups at my school library, but in reality I'd be with Billy. I never told him what happened to me after he was kicked out of my house.

Wela knew that Billy and I were friends. She would always invite him and me over to her home, a 3 floors, 8 bedrooms, 5 baths villa my Welo left for her along with millions.

Welo, real name Juneau, was a loveable grandfather. I only knew him for a little bit but the little bits I do remember will forever stay in my heart: him teaching me to read, the smell of newspaper in his room, watching the stooges with him, and that famous tagline of his "O". He passed away four years ago. His last words to me were, "Fly high and don't let anyone cut your wings. You will always be my fairy."

I answered, "O."

He gave me the Welo wink.

Her home was my Disney. Her home housed my TINKERBELL room. Glitter walls, a fluffy bed, fairy wing canopy, cupcake scented air, and I'd tell you more about it but I don't want you copying it.

caught up in the moment

School vacations were the best. Nathan was never around because he would hang out with the other rejects from the youth program at "Hell Central". That was fine with me because that meant I could spend lots of time with my pudding boy. Wela knew about me being gay, but she didn't know about Billy being my boyfriend. One day we were out back by the pool and Billy wanted to see me with my shirt off. So I took it off. Wela was inside fixing

herself a drink. Billy gasped.

"What?" I looked at myself and I

totally had forgotten about the bruises

Lucif-ather gave me the other day,

because he saw me in the Barbie isle at

the Wal-Mart where he worked.

"Caleb, were you in a fight or

something?"

"No Billy and I don't want to

talk about it. Now let's go swimming."

Billy held me back. He gently

outlined the bruises with his fingers and

it hurt.

I flinched.

"Did your dad hit you?"

"Don't go there!"

"Did he?"

"Billy please don't, let's just have fun before the summer is over."

Wela slammed the backdoor shut.

"Puchito! What are those marks doing on your back and don't lie to me!"

"Umm." I didn't know what to say and looked at Billy for help. Billy did the 'I don't know' shrug.

"Well, where'd you get those from," she said as she pointed to my bruises. "If Billy here likes it rough, I understand." She winked at Billy.

"Wela!"

Billy's blue eyes bulged out. "Ma'am I would never hurt your grandson."

"I know Billy, I'm just playing with you, but Puchito, where did you get those bruises from since you don't play sports?"

"Wela don't get mad, but it's," I

started to say but couldn't finish.

"His dad!" Billy yelled out.

Wela dropped her glass of

coquito and about faced. She went back

inside and all you heard was yelling.

ticket out

of hell

48

June 2, 2000. I'll never forget that day.

Verbal fights. Quick goodbyes. The happiest day of my life.

Wela chewed her son, my Lucif-ather, out and ripped him a new one.

She told him, "If he wants to suck dick let him suck dick!"

Roughly translated.

My jaw dropped.

My father shut up for the first time ever.

She also told him that there was

an eleventh commandment.

"THOU SHALL NOT FUCK WITH MY GRANDCHILDREN!"

Amen to that.

Wela pointed at my step-mom. "Like your wife, life's a bitch and then you die."

My stepmother ignored her because she was text messaging.

Wela slapped him, put me in the car, picked up Billy from his house and took us to her villa.

"So how'd it go?" Billy asked

over Elvis Crespo's 'Suavemente'

playing on the radio as my grandmother

was trying to sing along.

"Let's just say that Lucifer is out

of my life and I get a chance at a new

beginning."

I started to cry.

"What's wrong?" Billy held me.

"I know you're staying for the

rest of the summer, but what about when

school starts in August?" I looked away,

out the window as the desert sand and

cactus flew by like splashes of green

paint. "What'll happen to us?"

"Well let's see," Billy turned my face to him and wiped away my tears and said, "I turn 18 in three weeks. That makes me an adult. I spoke to my parents and to your grandmother and guess who is moving in with you?"

"Shut up!"

Billy smiled back at me and I kissed him forgetting that Wela was in the front seat driving. I didn't even notice that the music had stopped.

Wela while driving always had

the habit of instead of using the rearview mirror to talk to you, she had to turn her whole body around. Eye contact is the key to any conversation.

"Wela is this true?"

"Como la mierda abajo de un zapato." Basically like shit under a shoe.

We all laughed. Yes Billy may be Irish, but who the hell doesn't know that mierda means shit?

So there we all were. Wela, 65, driving, was dancing in her seat, and occasionally turned around to talk to us.

We almost crashed three times. Billy, soon to be 18 and holding the love of his life. Me, on the edge of 17, smiling for the first time, leaving HELL behind, secretly fondling Billy, and thinking of what the fuck to get for his birthday. The best road trip ever.

unconditional

Wela loved Billy. She knew that he loved me and that he would always take care of me. Wela was psychic like that. She told my father when he met Ineez, pronounced *cunt* and sometimes *step-bitch*, things would go to hell. I have to say they did.

"Puchito, I love the way you are. You don't hide, hold on...BINGO!"

She won three that night. The

thing I liked about her was her honesty and big heart. She would always give five dollars to the person next to her and always tell me, "Because you never know if that person will save your life one day."

I won twenty dollars, so I gave Wela five dollars. "Gracias, mi hijo," she said.

"Thanks for saving me Wela. Te quiero mucho."

I hugged her and she kissed my forehead.

Twenty minutes later.

"So Puchito, when Billy ask for sex does he want top or bottom?"

"Wela!"

We started to laugh and out of nowhere someone screamed bingo.

"Carajo!" Wela hollered.

The winner gave Wela the finger.

"Que te cages en la madre que te pario!" Wela said scolding at her.

I tried to change the subject while we were getting ready for the "Letter X" portion; basically you had to make an X on the bingo card.

"Wela, why does papi and ma hate Billy and me?"

She scanned her ten bingo cards and looked over at me with sad eyes.

"You see…hold on," she marked the other number, "the church your parents go to taught them to hate sinners. In their eyes you and Billy are sinners because you both like dick. Hell that makes me a sinner too. Shit, I missed a number. Dammit!"

She never really finished her

thought after this game because it was a

jackpot round. Wela adjusted her seat,

took a sip of Malta, looked at me and

said the most beautiful thing ever, "An

open mind creates an open heart to love.

No matter what bullshit you believe in."

"BINGO PUTA!" Wela

screamed.

I laughed.

The old lady who won a while

back, flicked Wela off.

Wela looked at me and said,

"Jodia vieja..."

I turned to pick up our bingo stuff. I heard screaming and realized that Wela had run up to the old lady that won and got in a fight with her. I had to hold her back.

"You saw her teeth fly out Puchito?" Wela said as she fixed her blue blouse.

"Yeah, but why did you attack her?" I tried to say in between laughs.

"La vieja me dio el birdie again," she said.

The old lady said something and

all I heard was, "Oh yeah porlomeno my

teeth are real puta!"

I laughed and got a text from Sherelle.

[I'm pregnant!]

I text messaged her back.

[I'm not surprised. You gonna be

on Maury? LOL]

Then she replied.

[Fuck you Caleb! LMAO!]

our quilt

After bingo I met Billy at Rosedale Park.

"Hey pudding!" I kissed him and sat down on a quilt he laid out on the grass. The corners brittle. Familiar to the touch. Torn yet hanging on stitch by stitch.

The spot at Rosedale Park was ours.

"You heard about Sherelle?" I asked.

"Yep," he told me as he played with my curls. "Phil told me."

The moonlight. The stars. The sweet smell of lavender.

Billy's body scent of the ocean engulfed my senses.

His warmth. Our spot.

"Wela got in a fight at bingo." I said as I snuggled in a little closer.

"What's new." Billy laughed. "Now kiss me."

Our quilt.

That evening as the lights went out, my eyes focused on the night sky through my bedroom window. There in our back yard floating in the darkness were elegant, mysterious golden lights.

The way they danced with the cool breeze was seductively sweet.

For hours my eyes stared at these magnificent floating lights. The essence of purity, each reminded me of star fairies.

Too bad they ended up being

fireflies.

Still, pretty at night, yet hard to catch in a jar, unlike memories.

xena joins us

Billy and I decided we needed some time to ourselves.

In June, we both graduated from high school and as a present, Wela let us borrow her car to head up to Las Vegas. She even told Billy one of her many wise quotes: "No me le rompas el culo la primera vez!" Basically, don't break my ass the first time.

As we headed up on our road trip

to Las Vegas, I knew that the most important decision of my life was about to be made. My mind was set. I knew what I wanted and more importantly I knew who I wanted to do the "Bicho Bicho" dance with. Now don't get me wrong, yes we've done other "stuff" with each other, I just haven't given Billy a golden ticket to my chocolate factory. Just realized that sounded wrong.

When we registered at the hotel, the lady at the front desk looked at Billy like he was some pervert with his whore anxious to fuck. She was half right. We went up to the room. It had a wooden dresser with a 16 inch silver TV, two twin beds with hippie yellow, neon green, blue colored covers, a mini-fridge and the room smelt like a fucking ashtray. Luckily I sprayed myself with Sweet Pea body splash which masked the scent.

"Oh, TV," was the first thing Billy said.

"I hope the beds are

comfortable." I took out my body splash and sprayed the place down. "Better?"

"Yep, come and sit next to me." Billy patted to a spot next to him on the bed.

The first thing I expected to do was to start ripping the clothes off of our backs. But I was so nervous. I sat next to Billy by the bed and took off my shoes. I was ready for it. He didn't seem to be as much.

"Oh cool, Xena is on," Billy said as he laid down on the bed.

All of a sudden I became nervous when Billy took off his shirt.

"Getting comfortable, that's it."

"Okay, I'll be right back." I got up and went to the bathroom. Don't get me started on how it looked.

I was hyperventilating. It's not because I didn't want to do it. Call it performance anxiety. This was the first time we'd actually go through with it. What if he didn't like it? What if it didn't get up or wasn't big enough to satisfy me? Holy shit! Was it too late to run out the door?

I came back and Billy was now lying in bed with no pants. Then he asked me if I wanted anything from the mini-fridge and I knew that he was doing the same thing I was … trying to stall the inevitable. Ok! This was ridiculous. We loved each other. So I started taking my clothes off. I laid down next to him. We kissed each other for a little while. Then we cuddled and kissed for a little more. Still stalling. Shit! Ok. We needed to do this. I moved to the edge of the bed and laid on my back.

Then Billy grabbed my legs and propped

them over his shoulders. His dick wasn't

cooperating. It wouldn't get hard. I got a

complex. Was I not attractive? Or was

Billy just nervous as hell?

"What's wrong Billy?"

"Mr. Happy isn't going up!"

I started to laugh. Which made

him laugh and the giggle attacks started.

We realized that it wasn't going to

happen. So we titty sucked and jacked

each other off. Our first time didn't go

the way I had expected it to go but one thing I knew for sure was that I didn't want to run away. Billy didn't either. That's how I knew it was true love.

baby momma

Four months later, Sherelle called me and said, "I finally gave birth to that little bitch!"

"Sherelle!" I started to laugh.

Billy was lying in bed sound asleep. We just had sex for the first time. I LOVED IT!

Thank "whoever the fuck made humans" that Wela won a bingo cruise trip to Mexico for a week. She would be back on my 18th b-day.

"Okay, so when you gonna come
and see this heathen of mine called
Coco?" Sherelle started to yell shut up to
her baby.

"How about we kill two birds
with one stone girl, I see your baby and
we celebrate my b-day next week at
Subways?" I put my Cookie Monster t-
shirt on and headed to the kitchen. "It
sounds like you want to spend some time
with Coco. Her screaming sounds
magical!" I snickered.

"Fuck you Caleb! You think you funny, huh?"

"Girl I am, and I have to tell you something too."

"You finally did it?"

"How'd you know?"

"I just know these things and I…..SHUT UP COCO!"

"Oh, let me let you go, I'll see you next week."

"How big was it?"

"Sherelle!"

I hung up and just in time. Billy

came in and wrapped his arms around me.

"I see Mr. Happy is up this time." I said as I poured hazelnut coffee into our matching lime-green mugs.

"He sure is," Billy said as he spun me around to face him. "What's for breakfast?"

I kissed him and said, "You are."

mr. happy

October 30, 2001. It was my birthday. Billy left early that morning for work at the local grocery store, Food Lion. He left me a rose and a note next to my pillow.

Dear Cupcake,

Roses are ruby red

Violets are baby blue

Tonight in bed

I will be loving you

(p.s. I wanted to say fucking but

it took away from the romance.)

Love Mr. Happy

I laughed and kissed the note.

I got dressed and headed to meet up with

Sherelle. On my walk there I got a call

from Wela. She told me she couldn't

make it back in time for my b-day. I told

her it was fine.

I got to Subways and walked in. I

gave Sherelle a hug and asked to see the

new addition.

"It's over there." She pointed to a stroller.

"Girl, why you were chosen to be a mother, who knows?"

"Caleb don't make me slap your ass!"

I laughed. Coco looked cute and still does, but enough about her.

"Now go order me my birthday sub, bitch!"

"Sure birthday cunt!"

We talked for a bit about her baby problems and I told her about Billy and my first night in Vegas.

"Caleb, that was way T.M.I. for me."

"Well you told me to spill all the details and I did."

Coco was quietly sleeping in her stroller.

"So, you never told me how big he was," Sherelle said.

"You tell me how big Phil is first."

I took a bite of my foot-long tuna sandwich.

"About that size," she said with a smirk.

I almost choked. I laughed so hard.

shit

Sherelle got a call on her cell phone. It was Billy. She handed the phone to me.

"Hello?"

"Honey, why haven't you picked up your phone?" Billy asked.

"I left it at home, why?"

"I've been trying to call you." Billy paused. "Something happened to

your grandma. Come home quick!"

"What?" I hung up the phone and told Sherelle I have to go.

"Hold on, I'll drive you home."

"Thanks, but hurry!"

"Damn bitch! You try lugging around 10 pounds of shit. Let me just get this lil'bitch in the car."

<u>oh no you didn't</u>

    Sherelle finally got me to my house. I was nervous as hell. Billy's car was in the driveway, but all the lights were off. Why have me come home and not to the hospital? Maybe she died and he doesn't want me to know.

    I got out of Sherelle's car and ran to the front door. I opened it and yelled for Billy.

    I turned on the foyer lights and

was greeted with people yelling,
"Surprise!"

I screamed like a little bitch and
threw myself on the floor to protect
myself.

"Caleb, you alright?" Billy knelt
down next to me.

"What the fuck is going on?" I
asked.

"Happy Birthday beautiful,"
Sherelle said as she came in from behind
me. "Awe shit! I forgot Coco."

"Feliz cumpleanos, Puchito

mio!" Wela picked me up and gave me a hug.

"You guys are assholes!" I said. "Here I thought Wela was dying."

"Por favor, el cabron ese me tiene que dar uno duro before he *kille* me!"

So there I was, 18, crying, thinking Wela was dead, Madison and Leila were partying in the Barbie playhouse watching Barbie's Next Top Model and I was having my first surprise birthday party ever.

Oh and the banner read, "Happy Birthday Bootiful!" Leave it to Wela to spell something.

***

Be on the lookout
for Z.C. Angel's
next project.

Whispering Poison

-a poetic novella-

Also stay up to date

with Z.C. Angel.

Twitter: @zcangel

Feedback is welcomed

nytecloude@hotmail.com